I0019396

Managing digital transformation strategies for success

Author:somayeh fakhraei

Somayeh Fakhraei

Table of Contents

Introduction

In today's fast - paced world, digital transformation is an important themes in management. With rapid technological advancements and markets constantly shifting , organizations increasingly need to adapt to these shifts. Digital transformation involves not only the adoption of new technologies but also deeper changes in organizational culture, business models, and customer relationships.

The aim of this book is to explore the challenges and opportunities arising from digital transformation and to provide strategies that help organizations succeed in this new era. We will examine the characteristics of effective leadership, practical strategies for implementing digital transformation, and real-world examples of organizations that have thrived on this journey.

Digital transformation is no longr an option; it is a necessity. Organizations must actively respond to customer needs using digital tools and data, making process with focus on optimization a processes. This book will offer insights to managers, leaders, and anyone seeking improvement and innovation, enabling them to progress along this path.

Let us embark on a journey to explore the world of digital transformation and the challenges and opportunities that lie ahead.

Reasons for Digital Transformation

Why is Digital Transformation Necessary?

By looking at the technological advancements in various industries, we realize that technology is constantly evolving. Organizations, businesses, and even our daily lives rely on these changes. Companies that fail to adapt quickly lose their competitive edge. This is where digital management becomes crucial.

Digital management helps organizations leverage new technologies, optimize processes, and enhance user and customer experiences. To better understand this, let's examine the evolution of technology across different industries:

The Evolution of Technology in Various Industries

1. Music & Entertainment

Cassette tapes → CDs → MP3 players → Digital downloads → Online streaming

Traditional cinemas → DVDs → Movie downloads → Streaming services

Offline video games → Online multiplayer games → Cloud gaming

2. Communication & Mobile Phones

Landline phones → Heavy mobile phones → Keypad mobile phones → Touchscreen smartphones → AI-powered mobile devices

SMS → Internet messaging apps → Video calls → AI chatbots

3. Transportation & Automobiles

Horse-drawn carriages → Manual cars → Automatic cars →

Electric cars → Self-driving vehicles

Paper maps → GPS devices → Smart navigation with real-time traffic updates

4. Shopping & Commerce

Traditional marketplaces → Chain stores → Online shopping → Voice-assisted and AI-powered shopping

Cash payments → Credit cards → Mobile payments → Digital currencies

5. Education & Learning

Chalkboards and chalk → Whiteboards and markers → Virtual classrooms → AI-driven and VR-based education

Printed books → E-books → Podcasts and online courses

How This Evolution Relates to Digital Management

These advancements show that technology never stops evolving, and businesses that fail to adapt are left behind.

Digital management helps organizations, schools, companies, and even daily life stay aligned with these rapid changes.In this chapter, we explore the key factors drivers that necessitate digital transformation in organizations. Understanding these reasons is crucial for stakeholders to fully recognize the importance of embracing digital strategies.

1. Changing Customer Behavior

The digital age has fundamentall   reshaped how consumers interact with brands and make purchasing decisions.

Expectations for Convenience: Customers expect seamless ,effortless experiences across all channels. They want to engage with brands through various platforms, including mobile apps, social media, and websites, often demanding quick responses and services. For example, Amazon has set new standards for convenience by offering a smooth experience from search to purchase and fast delivery..

personalization: Today's consumers seek personalized experiences tailored to their preferences. Organizations must leverage data analytics to understand customer behaviors and provide relevant recommendations and offerings.. Amazon's recommendation system, for instance, suggests products based on users' browsing and purchasing history, creating a highly personalized experience.

Access to Information: With vast information available online, customers are more informed than ever. They compare products, read reviews, and research options before making decisions. This shift necessitates that businesses be transparent and provide value to gain trust.

2. Intense Competition

The digital landscape has intensified competition across industries.

Emergence of Disruptive Startups: Startups often leverage digital technologies to disrupt traditional business models, challenging established players. Companies must innovate continually to maintain market share.

Global Reach: Digital platforms allow businesses to compete on a global scale. Organizations face competitors not only locally but also internationally, requiring them to enhance their offerings and differentiate themselves.

Rapid Technological Advancements: Technology evolves rapidly, and organizations that fail to adapt risk becoming obsolete. Staying ahead of technological trends is crucial for maintaining a competitive edge.

3. Increased Efficiency

Digital transformation offers significant opportunities for improving operational efficiency.

Automation of Processes: Automating repetitive tasks can streamline operations and reduce human error. This not only saves time but also allows employees to focus on higher-value activities. New technologies like artificial intelligence (AI) and robotics can automate many manual and time-consuming processes. For example, Amazon's warehouses are equipped with robots that speed up order processing and reduce operational costs.

Data-Driven Decision Making: Organizations can utilize data analytics to make informed decisions, optimize processes, and enhance performance. Real-time data can lead to faster responses and better outcomes.

Optimizing Supply Chains: Digital tools enable real-time monitoring and management of supply chains, leading to reduced waste and improved productivity. Amazon's sophisticated inventory management and same-day delivery systems are prime examples of supply chain optimization through digital transformation

Cost Reduction: Digital tools can help organizations cut costs by improving resource management and minimizing waste. This financial efficiency can lead to reinvestment in growth initiatives.

4. Regulatory Compliance

As digital technologies grow, so do regulations around how they can be used .

Data Privacy Laws: Regulations such as GDPR require organizations to manage customer data responsibly. Embracing digital transformation helps companies stay compliant while enhancing data security.

Industry Standards: Many industries have specific regulations that demand technological compliance. Digital transformation enables organizations to meet these standards efficiently.

5. Innovation and Growth Opportunities

Digital transformation opens new avenues for innovation and growth.

New Business Models: Organizations can explore innovative business models, such as subscription services, freemium offerings, or platform-based ecosystems, that leverage digital technologies.

Enhanced Customer Engagement: Digital tools facilitate better engagement with customers, enabling organizations to foster loyalty and build long-term relationships.

Market Expansion: Embracing digital transformation allows organizations to enter new markets more easily, reaching customers who may have been inaccessible through traditional channels.

Chapter 1

Challenges of Digital Transformation

Digital transformation presents organizations with a myriad of challenges that can impede their progress. Understanding these obstacles is crucial for successful implementation. In this chapter, we will explore some of the primary challenges organizations face:

1.1 Organizational Culture

A significant barrier to digital transformation is often the existing organizational culture. Resistance to change is common, as employees may be comfortable with established processes and hesitant to adopt new technologies. This inertia can slow down or even derail transformation efforts.

Example: At company "Anthony and Friends," employees were accustomed to traditional processes and resisted using new software, causing delays in digital projects.

1.2 Skill Gaps

The rapid evolution of technology necessitates a workforce equipped with the latest skills. Many organizations face skill gaps, where existing employees may lack the necessary digital competencies. Investing in training and development is essential but can be resource-intensive.

Example: The company realized that its marketing team lacked sufficient knowledge in digital marketing, prompting them to conduct training sessions.

1.3 Legacy Systems

Many organizations operate on outdated legacy systems that are incompatible with modern technologies. Transitioning from these systems can be complicated, requiring significant investment and time. The challenge lies in integrating new solutions without disrupting ongoing operations.

Example: "Anthony and Friends" faced coordination issues among teams due to reliance on outdated project management software, necessitating investment in new systems.

1.4 Leadership and Vision

Effective leadership is vital for driving digital transformation. Without a clear vision and commitment from the top management, initiatives may lack direction and support. Leaders must champion change and inspire their teams to embrace digital transformation.

Example: Leadership in the company lacked a clear vision for digital transformation, leading to confusion among employees regarding new goals.

1.5 Customer Expectations

As digital technologies evolve, customer expectations also shift. Organizations must adapt to these changing demands quickly, which can be a daunting task. Failing to meet customer expectations can lead to a loss of competitive advantage.

Example: Customers of "Anthony and Friends" expected fast and responsive services, but the inability to provide online services resulted in losing many of them.

Chapter 2

Leadership in the Digital Age

How AI is Transforming Leadership

1. Introduction to AI and Leadership Transformation Artificial Intelligence (AI) is dramatically reshaping leadership across industries. It's changing how leaders make decisions, manage teams, and approach strategy. By analyzing massive amounts of data, AI empowers leaders to make informed decisions, predict trends, and optimize resources more efficiently.

2. AI Enhancing Decision-Making One of the most significant ways AI is transforming leadership is by enhancing decision-making processes. With the help of machine learning and data analytics, AI tools can process data faster than humans, identify patterns, and offer insights that might have been overlooked. This allows leaders to make more accurate, data-driven decisions, reducing the risks associated with traditional, intuition-based leadership.

3. Changing Leadership Styles AI is shifting leadership styles from traditional, hierarchical structures to more collaborative, data-driven, and decentralized decision-making. With AI handling routine administrative tasks and providing data insights, leaders can focus more on high-level strategy, innovation, and human interaction. This shift allows leaders to become more forward-thinking, focusing on long-term goals instead of getting bogged down by day-to-day operations.

4. AI's Role in Resource Management AI is also revolutionizing how leaders manage resources, from time and money to human talent. By using AI-driven tools, leaders can predict resource needs, allocate them more efficiently, and monitor project progress in real-time. AI helps identify gaps in talent or resources, enabling leaders to optimize team structures and workflows, ultimately leading to better performance and outcomes.

5. The Evolution of Leadership Qualities As AI takes over more operational tasks, human leaders will need to focus on areas where AI falls short, like emotional intelligence, creativity, and ethical decision-making. AI can assist with analysis, but it cannot replace the ability to inspire, motivate, and empathize with teams. Leaders will increasingly need to blend technological knowledge with human qualities to remain effective in the AI-enhanced environment.

6. Ethical Considerations and AI Leadership The integration of AI in leadership does come with challenges, particularly around ethics. As AI systems become more autonomous, concerns regarding bias, transparency, and accountability arise. Leaders must ensure that AI systems are implemented ethically, ensuring fairness and avoiding discriminatory outcomes. This requires a delicate balance between leveraging technology and maintaining human oversight.

7. AI in Performance Management and Rewards

Artificial Intelligence plays a significant role in improving performance management and reward systems. One of the ongoing challenges for leaders is accurately evaluating employee performance and allocating rewards based on that. The use of AI can greatly enhance this process.

Performance Management With the help of AI systems, leaders can gather accurate data about employee performance. This data includes metrics such as time management, productivity, work quality, and project outcomes. AI can analyze this data and identify performance patterns that might be difficult for leaders to spot. As a result, leaders can make better decisions about promotions, career development, or adjustments to work strategies.

Rewards and Motivation AI also helps create more efficient reward systems. Rather than relying on generalized or unclear criteria, AI can allocate rewards based on actual employee performance, progress toward goals, and desired behaviors. This approach is more fair and transparent and can create stronger motivations for employees.

For example, AI-driven systems can assist leaders in assigning rewards that are personalized to individual needs and desires, such as training opportunities, financial bonuses, or increased responsibilities. These tailored rewards not only boost employee motivation and satisfaction but also enhance team efficiency.

The Future of AI in Leadership The future of leadership will be defined by the increasing presence of AI in decision-making and strategy. Leaders will rely on AI not just to manage operations but to predict market trends, understand consumer behavior, and improve organizational structures. AI will continue to assist leaders in making complex decisions, but the human element will remain indispensable in ensuring that these decisions align with values, ethics, and long-term vision.

In the era of digital transformation, effective leadership is critical for driving digital transformation. Leaders play a pivotal role in guiding organizations through change and fostering an environment conducive to innovation. This chapter examines the key characteristics of successful leaders in the digital age.

2.1 Visionary Thinking

Successful leaders have a clear vision of what digital transformation entails for their organization. They can communicate this vision to inspire and motivate their teams. A clear vision helps align the organization's efforts and provides a roadmap for implementation.

Example: The CEO of "Anthony and Friends" had a clear vision for digitizing the business, which motivated the team towards innovation.

2.2 Encouraging Innovation

Leaders need to create a culture of innovation where innovation is encouraged, experimentation is welcomed and failure is viewed as a learning opportunity. This mindset allows teams to explore new ideas and solutions without fear of repercussions.

Example: The company fostered an environment where new ideas were encouraged, leading to the introduction of new products that met customer needs.

2.3 Communication Skills

Effective communication is essential for leaders during times of change. They must clearly and consistently communicate the importance of digital transformation and its benefits . Open lines of communication help to reduce concerns employee and gain employee buy-in.

Example: Managers at "Anthony and Friends" built trust among employees by regularly and transparently communicating about digital changes.

2.4 Agility and Adaptability

In a rapidly changing digital landscape, leaders need to be agile and adaptable. This involves being open to new ideas, responding quickly to shifts, and making informed decisions based on data-driven insights.

Example: During a health crisis, the company quickly expanded its online services to keep up with market changes

2.5 Empowering Teams

Empowering teams is a hallmark of effective leadership. Leaders should delegate responsibilities, encourage collaboration, and provide their teams with the resources they need to succeed. This empowerment fosters a sense of ownership and accountability among employees.

Example: Managers at "Anthony and Friends" increased motivation and creativity among employees by granting them more autonomy.

2.6 Ethics in Organizational Leadership in the Digital Age

A leader in any organization must be proactive in establishing rules that align with the rapid pace of digital advancement. These rules should be designed to prevent potential abuses, ensuring that no individual takes unethical actions in the pursuit of profit. One such issue frequently discussed today is the sale of personal customer data, which requires specific regulations within the organization.

Ethics in an organization reflects the organization itself. Customers often form their perception of a company based on the ethical conduct of its employees and leadership. In the digital age, and in a competitive world, ethics remain a crucial factor. Leaders must not only ensure ethical practices but also serve as role models for their employees.

There are broad definitions of ethics, but what is important is that every organizational leader should consider this: failing to maintain ethical standards can lead to internal challenges, a loss of employee trust, and ultimately result in costly turnover and project delays due to the need for training new staff.

A strong ethical framework is essential for sustaining long-term success and maintaining a positive organizational reputation, especially in an era where digital transformation and data privacy are critical. As technology advances, ethical challenges also increase. Organizations must pay attention to issues such as data privacy, cybersecurity, and fair use of data, developing appropriate policies to address these matters.

Chapter 3

Strategies for Digital Transformation

Digital transformation requires careful planning and right strategies to achieve desired outcomes. In this chapter, we will explore key strategies for success in digital transformation.

3.1 New Business Models

Digital transformation often lead to changes in business models. Organizations must seek to identify new and innovative opportunities to create greater value for customers such as developing new products and services, establishing digital distribution channels, and enhancing customer interaction.

Example: Anthony and Friends" transformed its business model by offering online consulting services, attracting new customers.

Example: A traditional clothing store expands its business by creating an online shopping website and offering virtual styling consultations to attract more customers.

3.2 Choosing the Right Technology

Selecting the right technologies is crucial for implementing digital transformation . Organizations must identify their needs and seek digital solutions that align with their overall goals , such as data management software, analytical tools, and automation systems.

Example: The company implemented an advanced customer relationship management (CRM) system to improve interactions with clients

3.3 Data-Driven decision-making

Using data Effectively in decision-making is key a component of digital transformation. Organizations must collect, analyze, and leverage data to identify trends and customer needs. This approach aids in creating personalized experiences for customers.

Example: By analyzing customer data, "Anthony and Friends" launched targeted marketing campaigns.

Example: An e-commerce business notices that most of its customers shop online in the evening. By analyzing this data, they decide to launch special discounts and marketing campaigns during peak shopping hours, increasing their sales.

3.4 Collaboration and Partnerships

In the digital age, collaboration and partnerships with other organizations can accelerate the transformation process. Working with startups, consultants, and other industry entities can provide organizations with new innovations and additional resources.

Example: A manufacturing company partners with an AI startup to integrate smart automation into its production process, increasing efficiency and reducing costs.

3.5 Experimentation and Learning

The process of digital transformation requires a culture of experimentation and learning. Organizations should test new ideas and learn from their results. This process can facilitate continuous improvement and better adaptation to changes.Digital transformation is an ongoing process, not a one-time change. Businesses must cultivate a culture of experimentation and learning, where new ideas are tested, and lessons from failures drive improvement.

Example: A restaurant introduces an online ordering app but notices that customers prefer to call instead. Based on this insight, they refine their digital strategy and integrate a simple one-click ordering system via messaging apps

Example: "Anthony and Friends" regularly tested new ideas and used the results to improve processes.

In addition to the aforementioned trends in digital transformation, one critical strategy for managing the process effectively is the implementation of ISO standards. ISO standards provide a structured framework that ensures consistency, quality, and compliance throughout the digital transformation journey. This strategy not only supports operational efficiency but also mitigates potential risks associated with digitalization, making it an invaluable tool for organizations navigating the complexities of digital change.

The Impact of ISO Implementation on Digital Transformation

Introduction: In today's rapidly evolving digital landscape, digital transformation has become a critical imperative for organizations. As businesses adopt digital technologies, shift to online platforms, and integrate data-driven processes, they face challenges in maintaining quality, security, and compliance. ISO standards, known for providing frameworks for quality management, play a crucial role in ensuring that digital transformation initiatives are successful. This chapter delves into how ISO standards impact digital processes, enhance operational efficiency, and enable organizations to manage risks and opportunities in the digital age.

The integration of ISO standards helps organizations establish a uniform approach to digital processes, safeguard data, and align with international regulations. This chapter will explore the benefits of implementing ISO standards and how they facilitate the digital transformation journey.

Key Questions in this Chapter:

1. How can ISO implementation standardize digital processes?

ISO standards such as ISO 9001 (Quality Management Systems) and ISO 22301 (Business Continuity Management) offer organizations the tools they need to standardize their operations, particularly in digital processes. The implementation of these standards ensures consistency, performance, and continual improvement, which are critical in maintaining high-quality digital services. By adhering to these standards, organizations can streamline operations, reduce errors, and increase the effectiveness of digital tools and platforms. This also creates a unified approach across different departments, which is particularly important in large, digitally transformed organizations.

2. Can ISO contribute to improving data security in the era of digital transformation?

Data security is one of the biggest concerns in digital transformation, as the increasing volume of data shared and stored online opens doors to potential security breaches. ISO standards like ISO 27001 (Information Security Management Systems) provide organizations with a systematic approach to managing sensitive information, mitigating data security risks, and ensuring compliance with regulations like GDPR (General Data Protection Regulation). By implementing ISO 27001, organizations can assess vulnerabilities in their digital processes, adopt best practices for data encryption, and ensure that all stakeholders, both internally and externally, follow secure practices. This improves trust among customers and partners, which is essential for long-term success.

3. What is the connection between ISO implementation and increased customer satisfaction in digital transformation?

ISO standards are deeply focused on customer satisfaction. For example, ISO 9001 places a strong emphasis on understanding and meeting customer requirements. When organizations implement ISO standards, they ensure that digital products, services, and interactions meet or exceed customer expectations. In a digital world, where customers demand seamless and efficient experiences, this is critical. By adhering to ISO standards, organizations can optimize their digital services, deliver on-time, improve usability, and respond effectively to customer feedback. These improvements in service delivery ultimately lead to higher customer satisfaction and increased loyalty.

4. How can ISO help organizations maintain compliance with digital regulations and laws?

As the digital world expands, so does the complexity of regulations that govern data privacy, security, and digital transactions. Adopting ISO standards enables organizations to stay compliant with both national and international regulations. For example, ISO 27001 helps ensure that an organization's information security policies are aligned with regulations such as the GDPR in the EU or the CCPA in California.

Compliance is not only about avoiding penalties but also about building a reputation for ethical business practices, which is especially important in the digital environment where customers are increasingly aware of data privacy concerns. ISO's role in helping organizations maintain this compliance mitigates the risk of legal issues, fines, and reputation damage.

5. How does ISO implementation in digital transformation contribute to enhancing an organization's competitive capabilities?

In the digital era, competition is fierce, and the ability to leverage technology efficiently is crucial. ISO implementation provides organizations with a competitive edge by streamlining processes, reducing inefficiencies, and improving service delivery. Standards such as ISO 9001 and ISO 14001 (Environmental Management Systems) help organizations innovate in their digital strategies, drive continuous improvement, and adopt a proactive approach to risk management. Additionally, organizations that adhere to ISO standards are often seen as more reliable and trustworthy by customers, partners, and stakeholders, which can help attract new business opportunities. The credibility gained from certification can be a decisive factor when consumers or clients compare digital service providers in a crowded marketplace.

ISO implementation serves as a powerful tool in managing the complexities of digital transformation. By providing a structured approach to quality management, data security, and compliance, ISO standards enable organizations to mitigate risks, enhance operational efficiency, and foster customer trust in their digital initiatives. The benefits of ISO implementation are far-reaching, from improving internal processes to gaining a competitive edge in the market. Organizations that invest in ISO standards as part of their digital transformation strategy are better positioned to succeed in an increasingly digital and interconnected world.

In conclusion, as digital transformation becomes the cornerstone of business success, ISO standards offer a framework that ensures organizations can navigate this shift effectively while maintaining quality, security, and compliance. By embedding ISO standards into their digital processes, organizations can enhance their long-term viability and thrive in the digital age.

chapter 4

Data Management and Analytics

Data plays a crucial role in the digital world, and effective management can enhance decision-making and organizational efficiency.   Effective data management and analysis help organizations optimize their operations, improve customer experiences, and drive innovation.In this chapter, we will discuss the importance of data and its analysis in the digital transformation process.

4.1 Importance of Data

Data is recognized as a primary source of information in the digital age. Organizations must pay special attention to collecting, storing, and analyzing data to improve their services and products.

Example: "Anthony and Friends" recognized that data serves as a primary source of information crucial for decision-making.

example: An online store noticed that more people bought sports gear on weekends. By analyzing this trend, they stocked up on popular items before the weekend rush, increasing sales.

4.2 Data Analytics Tools

Utilizing data analytics tools helps organizations understand customer behavior and market trends. Analytical tools such as Business Intelligence (BI) and machine learning help in identifying patterns and predicting customer behavior.

Example: A restaurant chain used data analytics to track customer preferences and found that people ordered more spicy dishes in colder months. They used this insight to launch a seasonal spicy menu, which boosted sales.

Example: The company utilized data analytics tools to identify customer purchasing patterns and develop better marketing strategies.

4.3 Process Optimization

Proper data management and analysis can contribute to the optimization of internal processes. Through data analysis, organizations can identify their strengths and weaknesses and take actions to improve efficiency.

Example: A manufacturing company analyzed production data and realized that a specific machine was slowing down operations. By upgrading it, they increased productivity by 20%.

Example: Through data analysis, "Anthony and Friends" optimized internal processes, increasing efficiency.

4.4 Privacy and Security Compliance

With the increased collection of data, privacy and security issues have become significant . Organizations must ensure that customer data is securely stored and managed while complying with privacy regulations.

Example: A financial services company introduced encrypted transactions and biometric logins to prevent fraud and safeguard user data.

Example: The company implemented appropriate security measures to ensure that customer data was stored and managed securely.

4.5 Data-Driven Culture

A data-driven mindset helps teams make smarter, fact-based decisions.Creating a data-driven culture within the organization is key to success in digital transformation. All team members should be aware of the importance of data and its analysis, actively using data for their decision-making processes.

Example: At "Anthony and Friends," all employees were encouraged to use data in their decision-making processes.

Example: A retail company encouraged all employees, from marketing to logistics, to rely on data for their decisions. This approach improved customer satisfaction and reduced unnecessary costs.

Chapter 5

Success Stories

In this chapter, we will examine real-world examples of organizations that have successfully undergone digital transformation. These case studies can provide insights into effective strategies and approaches.

5.1 Case Study 1: Amazon

Amazon is one of the most successful examples of digital transformation. The company has optimized the online shopping experience by leveraging data and innovative technologies. As a multifaceted platform, Amazon not only sells products but also offers services like Amazon Prime and AWS (Amazon Web Services). This diversity in services and the use of data for personalizing customer experiences have contributed significantly to Amazon's success.

Amazon's Digital Transformation: A Masterclass in Innovation and Leadership

From Bookstore to Tech Giant

In 1994, Jeff Bezos started Amazon as an online bookstore, but he had a much bigger vision. He saw the potential of the internet and understood that technology could reshape the way people shop. Fast forward to today, and Amazon is no longer just an e-commerce company—it's a leader in cloud computing, artificial intelligence, logistics, and digital services.

But how did Amazon achieve this? The answer lies in bold leadership, relentless customer focus, and an unwavering commitment to innovation. This chapter explores how Amazon leveraged digital transformation to build one of the most powerful companies in the world.

Customer-First: The Driving Force Behind Amazon's Digital Transformation

Unlike many companies that focus on their competition, Amazon's strategy has always been simple: obsess over the customer. Every major decision, from Prime's two-day shipping to Alexa's voice shopping, stems from this principle.

-Personalized Shopping with AI

Amazon doesn't just sell products; it anticipates what customers want before they even know it. Thanks to sophisticated AI-driven recommendation engines, Amazon suggests products based on browsing history, past purchases, and even what other users with similar interests have bought. This isn't just smart marketing—it's digital transformation at its best.

-Seamless and Frictionless Shopping

From one-click purchasing to same-day delivery, Amazon continuously reduces friction in the shopping experience. The goal? To make buying as effortless as possible. And it works—customers keep coming back.

-The Tech That Powers Amazon's Success

Amazon Web Services (AWS): The Engine Behind the Digital World

Amazon's biggest success story isn't even its online store—it's AWS. Originally built to handle Amazon's internal infrastructure, AWS evolved into the leading cloud computing provider, powering everything from Netflix to NASA.

The impact of AWS on digital transformation is massive:

Scalability – Startups and enterprises can access computing power on demand.

AI & Machine Learning – AWS tools help companies develop AI-driven applications.

Cost Efficiency – Businesses save millions by avoiding expensive IT infrastructure.

-Automation and AI in Amazon's Warehouses

Ever wondered how Amazon delivers millions of packages so quickly? The secret lies in its highly automated warehouses, where AI and robots handle everything from sorting products to predicting demand.

Robotics streamline order fulfillment, speeding up deliveries.

Predictive analytics ensure the right products are stocked in the right locations.

AI-driven logistics optimize supply chain efficiency, reducing costs and waste.

Alexa: AI in Everyday Life

Amazon's digital transformation isn't just about warehouses—it's in people's homes. Alexa, Amazon's voice assistant, is a prime example of how AI is shaping consumer behavior. With Alexa, customers can shop, control smart home devices, and even ask for the weather—completely hands-free.

-Leadership and Organizational Culture

The "Day 1" Mentality

Jeff Bezos often talks about Amazon's "Day 1" philosophy, which means always operating with the urgency and innovation of a startup. The idea is simple: the moment a company becomes too comfortable, it stops growing.

-Decentralized Teams for Rapid Innovation

Amazon is structured in a way that allows small, independent teams to work on new ideas. This decentralized approach encourages faster decision-making and experimentation, leading to groundbreaking innovations.

-Challenges and The Road Ahead

Regulatory and Ethical Concerns

As Amazon grows, so do its challenges. Governments worldwide are scrutinizing its business practices, from data privacy to labor policies. Managing this balance between innovation and regulation will be key to its future success.

Web3, Blockchain, and The Future of Digital Commerce

Looking ahead, Amazon may embrace blockchain technology for secure transactions, Web3 for decentralized commerce, and even the metaverse for virtual shopping experiences. The next phase of digital transformation is just beginning.

-Lessons from Amazon

Amazon's journey proves that digital transformation isn't just about adopting new technology—it's about mindset, leadership, and relentless customer focus. Businesses looking to thrive in the digital era can learn from Amazon's approach:

1. Always put the customer first.

2. Invest in AI and automation.

3. Create a culture of continuous innovation.

5.2 Case Study 2: Nike

Nike, a well-known sports brand, has improved customer experience by embracing digital transformation and utilizing new technologies. The company collects data related to users' sports activities through apps and wearable devices, providing them with insights to enhance their performance. This approach has enabled Nike to establish a closer connection with its customers and strengthen its brand.

A fictional company, "Anthony & Friends," illustrates the potential of digital transformation in a service-oriented industry. By implementing a comprehensive customer relationship management (CRM) system, they personalized communication with clients, leading to a 30% increase in customer retention. Their use of data analytics to understand customer preferences enabled them to tailor services effectively, resulting in higher satisfaction rates.

5.3 Lessons from Failures

In addition to successes, examining examples of organizations that have failed in digital transformation is also important.

Companies like Blockbuster, which could not adapt to rapid market changes and continued to follow outdated business models, serve as good examples of such failures. These cases can teach organizations the necessity of adaptability and innovation.

Examples of Failure and Their Causes

1. Failure of a Tech Startup

Example: A company launched a mobile app for time management, but it shut down after a year.

Reasons for Failure:

Lack of Market Research: The company didn't analyze users' real needs, and the app had overly complex features that most users didn't require.

Strong Competition: Well-established apps like Trello and Google Calendar already dominated the market.

Financial Issues: The startup lacked sufficient investment and couldn't cover marketing and development costs.

2. Failure of a Writer in Selling Books

Example: A writer published their first novel, but sales were extremely low.

Reasons for Failure:

Ineffective Marketing: The writer only published the book without a proper marketing strategy.

Unattractive Cover and Title: The book's cover was not appealing, and the title was confusing for readers.

Lack of Audience Understanding: The book was in a highly competitive genre, but the writer didn't research the target audience well.

3. Failure of a Sports Team in an International Competition

Example: A football team, expected to win the championship, was eliminated in the first round.

Reasons for Failure:

Poor Physical Preparation: Due to improper training schedules, players were not in top physical condition.

Weak Coaching Strategies: The team's tactics were ineffective, failing to exploit opponents' weaknesses.

Psychological Pressure: Players were under immense pressure from media and fans, which negatively affected their performance.

4. Failure in Digital Transformation

Example: A traditional company attempted to modernize its systems through digital transformation but failed despite significant investments.

Reasons for Failure:

Employee Resistance: The staff resisted change because they lacked proper training.

Choosing the Wrong Technology: The company implemented overly complex tools that were difficult to use.

Lack of Clear Planning: The transformation process started without a well-defined roadmap and was eventually abandoned.

5. Failure of an Environmental Project

Example: A group of activists launched a campaign to reduce plastic waste, but it had little impact.

Reasons for Failure:

Lack of Public Awareness: People did not fully understand the importance of the issue.

No Government Support: There were no laws or incentives to encourage plastic reduction.

Ineffective Advertising Methods: The campaign's messaging was not engaging or persuasive enough.

All these failures may have other reasons, but they should be used as opportunities for success and strengthening weaknesses. By analyzing what went wrong, one can identify key areas for improvement, learn from mistakes, and apply those lessons to future endeavors. Failures are valuable learning experiences that can guide better decision-making, foster innovation, and ultimately lead to greater success.

Chapter 6

The Future of Digital Transformation

In this chapter, we will explore future trends and challenges in the realm of digital transformation. Understanding these trends can help organizations prepare for what lies ahead.

6.1 Future Trends

The future of digital transformation will be shaped by technological advancements such as artificial intelligence, machine learning, the Internet of Things (IoT), and blockchain. These technologies will not only change business practices but will also transform how organizations interact with customers.

6.2 Preparing for the Future

Organizations must actively prepare for the future. This includes investing in new technologies, training and developing employee skills, and fostering a culture of innovation. Additionally, organizations should seek new partnerships and collaborations to leverage the benefits of emerging technologies.

6.3 Predicting Market Changes

In the digital age, the ability to predict market changes and customer needs is of paramount importance. Organizations should continuously analyze data to identify trends and patterns, allowing them to respond quickly to changes.

Chapter 7

Fostering Digital Transformation

Key Insights for Success

Digital transformation is more than just a buzzword these days—it's become essential for organizations looking to stay competitive and thrive in an increasingly fast-paced world. But what does it really take to manage a successful digital transformation? Based on recent research and real-world examples, we've uncovered several key insights that can guide organizations through this complex journey.

7.1. The Power of Strategic Alignment

One of the most important takeaways from the research is how critical it is for digital initiatives to align with the overall business strategy. A staggering 85% of participants in the study highlighted that when digital transformation is closely tied to the company's core goals, it significantly boosts the chances of success. When organizations have a clear vision of how technology can support their mission and business objectives, they are far more likely to see positive results.

Think about it this way: if you're driving a car, it's not enough just to have a powerful engine. You also need to know where you're going. The engine is the technology, but the map is the strategy. Without the right direction, even the most advanced tools can fall short.

7.2. Building a Digital-First Culture

Another crucial insight is the importance of creating a digital-first culture. In today's fast-evolving digital landscape, it's not enough to simply adopt new technologies. You need to build an environment where people within the organization embrace change, continue learning, and are motivated to innovate. In fact, 92% of the leaders interviewed stressed that fostering a culture that values digital literacy and continuous development is vital for transformation.

Creating a digital culture is more than just implementing new software or tools. It's about changing mindsets. When employees are engaged, when they feel that digital transformation is not something imposed on them but a part of their growth and opportunity, the transition becomes smoother and more effective. Investing in leadership training, workshops, and team-building exercises can go a long way in helping your workforce feel confident and ready for change.

7.3 Centralized Teams: The Glue That Holds It Together

Many organizations find that managing digital transformation efforts across multiple departments can get messy. That's why the research found that having a centralized digital transformation unit makes a world of difference. A dedicated team focused on overseeing and aligning digital initiatives ensures that efforts aren't fragmented, making the transformation process much more cohesive and efficient.

Think of this centralized team as the orchestrator of a symphony. Every department plays its part, but the central team ensures that all the instruments come together harmoniously. This leads to a more streamlined approach, where resources are effectively allocated, and no department is left behind in the transformation process.

7.4 Integrating the Right Technology

It's clear that technology is at the heart of digital transformation. AI, cloud computing, and data analytics are no longer just nice-to-haves—they're essential tools for improving operations and enhancing customer experience. The research showed that companies that successfully integrated these technologies saw remarkable improvements, including a 30-40% increase in customer satisfaction and a 25% reduction in operational costs.

In today's world, having access to data is like having a compass on a journey. It guides decisions, helps organizations better understand their customers, and drives innovation. But it's not enough to just collect data—you need to know how to use it. Companies that truly embrace data-driven strategies can anticipate customer needs, optimize processes, and stay one step ahead of their competitors.

Why Does All This Matter?

So, why is all of this important? Simply put, because the world is changing fast. Customers expect instant gratification and seamless digital experiences. Competition is no longer just local —it's global. And technology is evolving at breakneck speeds, meaning that businesses that don't adapt risk falling behind.

By aligning your digital efforts with your business strategy, fostering a culture that embraces technology, centralizing your transformation efforts, and integrating the right technologies, you put your organization in a much stronger position to succeed in the digital age.

Practical Tips for Navigating Digital Transformation

If you're in the midst of a digital transformation—or if you're just getting started—here are a few practical tips:

Get buy-in from leadership: It's essential that leadership is not only on board with digital transformation but also actively driving it. Their commitment will inspire others to follow suit.

Invest in people, not just technology: Technology alone won't make you successful. Make sure your team has the skills and knowledge they need to use new tools effectively.

Keep the customer in mind: Digital transformation isn't just about internal processes—it's about enhancing the customer experience. Always ask yourself: how will this change benefit our customers?

Don't be afraid to start small: Big changes can be overwhelming. Consider starting with a small pilot project before scaling up to a full-fledged transformation.

Looking Ahead: What's Next?

The world of digital transformation is still evolving, and there's so much more to learn. The future is likely to bring even more advanced technologies, like AI, blockchain, and the Internet of Things (IoT), which will continue to reshape industries. Staying ahead of the curve will require continuous investment in technology and talent. But more importantly, it will require a commitment to creating a culture that welcomes change, values innovation, and sees transformation as an ongoing process, not a one-time event.

Digital transformation is not an option anymore; it's a necessity. But success doesn't come easily. It requires a strategic approach that aligns your digital efforts with your business goals, builds a culture of innovation, and integrates the right technologies in the right way. By focusing on these key areas, organizations can navigate the complexities of digital transformation and unlock its full potential.

Chapter8

Steps for Implementing Digital Transformation

Implementation of Digital Transformation

In implementing digital transformation, we must remember that management is still rooted in the same four fundamental principles: Planning, Organizing, Leading, and Controlling. The key to success lies in applying these principles effectively, even as we navigate the challenges of the digital age. In this section, we will take each step of the digital transformation process and align it with these core management principles.

1. Planning Digital Transformation

-Define Clear Objectives

Establishing clear goals and outcomes for the digital transformation initiative is essential. These objectives must align with the organization's broader strategy. By setting specific, measurable, and achievable goals, we can provide direction and ensure that every action taken during the transformation aligns with the long-term vision.

-Assess Current Capabilities

A comprehensive analysis of current technologies, processes, and skills is needed to identify strengths and gaps. This assessment enables the organization to understand where it stands and what resources will be required for the transformation.

Example: A Small Business Transitioning to E-Commerce

Imagine a small family-owned bakery that has been operating traditionally for decades. The bakery owner, Maria, realizes that in order to keep up with changing times and customer expectations, she must adopt an online platform. So, she sets clear objectives: increasing her sales by 30% within the next year through online orders, and broadening her reach to customers beyond the local area.

Maria also takes time to assess her current capabilities: the bakery doesn't have a website, the staff isn't familiar with digital tools, and the inventory management is done manually. She then establishes a plan to integrate e-commerce, hire a web developer, and train her staff in digital tools.

This step of planning is key to ensuring the transition is purposeful and aligned with the bakery's vision, despite being a small-scale operation

2. Organizing Digital Resources

-Engage Stakeholders

Organizing the digital transformation process involves bringing in all key stakeholders, from leadership to employees and customers, to ensure their support and involvement. By identifying the right team members and resources, organizations can create an efficient framework for executing the transformation.

-Develop a Roadmap

Once the right team is in place, a clear roadmap must be developed. This detailed plan should outline the necessary steps, timelines, and resources to achieve the transformation. It ensures that everyone is on the same page and moving in the same direction.

-Invest in Technology

As part of the organizing phase, investing in the right technologies is crucial. This includes implementing cloud solutions, data analytics, and automation tools that will support the organization's goals and enhance overall efficiency.

Example: Empowering Employees to Embrace Digital Tools

Next, Maria organizes her resources. She brings together her employees—ranging from the bakers to the cashier—and helps them understand the importance of adopting new technologies. She ensures they feel included in the process by actively seeking their feedback on what tools they think would improve efficiency.

She develops a clear roadmap: first, launching the website, second, integrating a payment system, and third, training the team on managing online orders. Maria invests in simple digital tools that her team can use daily—like inventory software and a social media scheduling tool for marketing.

This approach to organizing not only improves efficiency but also fosters a sense of ownership among her employees, making them feel part of the transformation

3. Leading Digital Transformation

-Foster a Culture of Innovation

Effective leadership is key to digital transformation. Leaders must create a culture that encourages innovation and experimentation. This involves inspiring employees to propose new ideas, try different approaches, and embrace digital tools to drive progress. A mindset of continuous learning and adaptation must be instilled at all levels.

-Provide Training and Support

For employees to succeed in the digital transformation process, they need the right training and support. By offering programs that develop their digital skills, leaders can ensure their teams are equipped to take full advantage of the new tools and processes.

Example: Leading by Example

As the leader, Maria must foster a culture of innovation. She encourages her team to experiment with new ideas, like offering online-only discounts or collaborating with local delivery services to expand her customer base. Maria leads by example—she makes sure to personally familiarize herself with the tools and platforms and demonstrates how they can enhance day-to-day operations.

When the website has a technical glitch or an order gets delayed, Maria remains calm, addresses the issue with the team, and turns it into an opportunity for learning rather than a failure. This helps create an open, experimental atmosphere where her employees feel safe to try new ideas and troubleshoot problems together.

By doing this, Maria is not only driving the bakery's transformation but also setting an example of resilience, adaptability, and the power of continuous improvement—key aspects of leading in the digital era

4. Controlling and Monitoring Progress

-Implement Changes Gradually

To minimize disruption and ensure smooth implementation, digital transformation should be rolled out in phases. This approach allows for adjustments based on feedback and results, making it easier to control the process and make necessary corrections.

-Measure and Evaluate Progress

Continuous monitoring is essential to assess the effectiveness of the digital transformation. By regularly reviewing performance metrics, organizations can determine whether they are on track and identify areas for improvement. Control mechanisms should be in place to make real-time adjustments as needed.

-Scale Successful Initiatives

Once initial changes have been successfully implemented, scaling them across the organization can maximize their impact. Expanding successful pilot projects and initiatives ensures the full benefits of digital transformation are realized across all departments and functions.

Example: Adjusting the Course Based on Feedback

After the bakery starts taking online orders, Maria realizes that some customers are struggling to navigate the website. Sales are lower than expected, and customers are abandoning their carts mid-purchase. Maria quickly collects feedback from her customers and her team, finding that the website's payment process is too complicated for many.

Maria responds by simplifying the checkout process, adding clearer instructions, and offering customer service training for her staff to assist clients who have issues with orders. She then monitors the progress by reviewing weekly sales and customer feedback to measure the effectiveness of the changes.

This approach to controlling ensures that Maria is actively adjusting the process based on real-time feedback, rather than waiting until the problem escalates. It shows how continuous evaluation and improvement are integral to the success of any digital transformation.Example: ABC Manufacturing Company – Digital Transformation Journey

Background: ABC Manufacturing, a mid-sized company in the production industry, has been operating for over 20 years. While its legacy systems have served the company well, it has recently faced challenges such as inefficiencies in production, poor resource allocation, and limited ability to scale. The management team recognizes that digital transformation is essential for staying competitive in the market.

Step 1: Planning the Digital Transformation

The management team begins by outlining a comprehensive digital transformation strategy. This plan includes the implementation of new technologies such as IoT for smarter production lines, machine learning algorithms for predictive maintenance, and ERP systems to streamline operations.

To ensure quality throughout this process, ABC decides to adopt the ISO 9001 quality management standard. They aim to achieve this certification by aligning their internal processes with ISO's requirements, ensuring that every stage of the transformation is structured and results in a consistent, high-quality outcome.

Step 2: Organizing for Success

To implement the transformation, ABC forms a specialized project team that includes representatives from the IT department, production managers, and quality assurance specialists. This cross-functional team is responsible for ensuring that digital tools are implemented effectively and that ISO 9001 standards are adhered to.

The company allocates resources to key areas:

Purchasing new machinery with integrated sensors.

Implementing cloud-based ERP systems.

Training employees on using new digital tools.

Step 3: Leading the Transformation

The CEO and senior leadership take an active role in driving the digital transformation. They communicate a clear vision of the company's future, where digital tools will enable efficiency, enhance quality, and improve decision-making.

To engage the workforce, leadership encourages open communication and emphasizes the benefits of adopting digital technologies. Managers hold regular workshops to train employees on the new systems, and leaders act as role models in embracing change.

Step 4: Controlling and Monitoring Progress

Once the digital systems are in place, ABC uses real-time dashboards and performance metrics to monitor the success of the transformation. The company tracks KPIs such as production efficiency, quality control metrics, and resource utilization.

Regular ISO 9001 audits are conducted to ensure the company's processes continue to meet the high standards required for certification. Any issues, such as delays in production or deviations from the quality standards, are immediately flagged and corrected.

For example, if a machine malfunctions, the predictive maintenance system alerts the team, preventing potential delays and reducing downtime. Additionally, customer satisfaction surveys are monitored to ensure the company is meeting the expectations set by the ISO 9001 quality standards.

Step 5: Results and Future Steps

After a year of digital transformation, ABC Manufacturing sees significant improvements:

Production efficiency has increased by 20%.

The company successfully receives ISO 9001 certification, demonstrating its commitment to quality.

The implementation of predictive analytics has reduced maintenance costs by 15%.

Encouraged by these results, ABC plans to further enhance its digital capabilities by exploring the integration of artificial intelligence and blockchain technology in its supply chain to ensure even greater transparency and efficiency in the future.

Through careful planning, organizing, leading, and controlling, along with a strong commitment to ISO 9001 standards, ABC Manufacturing has successfully navigated its digital transformation. The company is now more efficient, competitive, and prepared for the challenges of the future.

Conclusion

Digital transformation is not merely a trend; it is a fundamental shift that organizations must embrace to remain competitive in an ever-evolving marketplace. In today's world, digital transformation has become an essential need for every business. As we saw in this book, this transformation not only refers to technological changes but also includes shifts in management styles and organizational processes. For a business to succeed in the digital age, managers must align themselves with technological changes and adopt new strategies to lead the organization effectively.

Managers have always worked within the framework of planning, organizing, leading, and controlling, but in today's digital world, this role has become a bit more complex and challenging. For example, managing human resources and business processes now requires the use of new technologies. Additionally, managers need the ability to make quick and accurate decisions in a digital world where information changes rapidly, and opportunities and threats emerge quickly.

ISO, as a management tool, helps managers standardize organizational processes, resulting in improved efficiency and quality. These standards help businesses operate effectively in their digital transformation process and respond to challenges.

however, technological changes are just part of digital transformation. One of the main challenges managers face is how to use technologies in the best possible way to improve processes, facilitate communication, and ultimately provide a better experience for customers.

digital transformation is a continuous process that never stops. Therefore, for businesses to succeed in this era, they must pay close attention to technological changes, digital strategies, and management standards. These changes may present challenges, but with proper management, they can create new opportunities and sustainable growth.The journey involves overcoming significant challenges, such as cultural resistance, skill gaps, and legacy systems, while leveraging effective leadership, innovative strategies, and data-driven decision-making.

Successful examples, such as Amazon and Nike, demonstrate the potential rewards of embracing digital transformation, providing valuable lessons and insights. However, organizations must also learn from failures to understand the importance of adaptability and ongoing innovation.

Looking to the future, emerging technologies will continue to shape the landscape of digital transformation. Organizations that proactively prepare for these changes, cultivate a data-driven culture, and address ethical challenges will be better positioned to thrive in the digital age.

Ultimately, the success of digital transformation depends on a holistic approach that encompasses not only technology but also people, processes, and a commitment to continuous improvement.

Challenges and Opportunities

Implementing digital transformation, especially in complex environments and large organizations, is not without its challenges. Many businesses face issues like resistance to change from employees, budget constraints, and lack of digital skills during their early stages of digital transformation. However, as discussed in this book, these challenges can be managed with the right strategies and effective change management.

At the same time, digital transformation presents numerous opportunities for businesses that are willing to embrace it. Digital advertising, as one of the key tools, enables companies to reach their target audience, build long-term relationships with customers, and ultimately increase their growth and profitability.

The Importance of ISO Implementation in This Process

One of the crucial aspects of digital transformation is the implementation of ISO standards. ISO, as a management tool, helps organizations standardize their processes, resulting in improved quality, efficiency, and transparency. These standards can assist organizations in various sectors, from human resource management to project management and digital marketing, enhancing their overall performance.

For an organization to succeed in its digital transformation process, it must pay particular attention to the proper implementation of these standards. ISO not only improves processes but also fosters a culture of continuous improvement, enabling organizations to operate more efficiently in the digital world and outperform their competitors.

Digital Transformation and the Future of Organizations

Finally, as we discussed in this book, digital transformation is a never-ending process. It is a continuous cycle of adopting new technologies, adapting to market changes, and innovating business models. In this journey, organizations must always stay up to date and prepare for the future.

or an organization to achieve sustained success, it must not only embrace new technologies but also focus on digital strategies, effective human resource management, targeted digital advertising, and ISO standards. This strategic combination across various aspects of digital transformation can propel businesses to superior positions in competitive markets.

Therefore, what is known today as digital transformation is no longer a choice but a necessity. Any business that aims to succeed in this digital age must integrate a mix of cutting-edge technologies, digital transformation management, and ISO standards into its strategies. This process will not only enhance efficiency and service quality but also elevate customer experience, improve stakeholder relationships, and ultimately drive growth and success in the market.

The Future

Preparing Children for the Digital World

As we look to the future, one of the most critical aspects of digital transformation is preparing the next generation to thrive in an increasingly digital world. Schools and educational systems play a pivotal role in equipping children with the necessary skills, knowledge, and mindset to succeed in this rapidly evolving environment.

1. Embracing Technology in Education:

Schools must integrate technology not only as a subject but as a tool to enhance learning across all subjects. By incorporating digital tools and platforms, children can develop essential skills such as problem-solving, critical thinking, and creativity. This technological integration should begin at an early age to ensure students become comfortable with digital tools and can use them effectively in their education.

2. Teaching Digital Literacy:

In the future, being digitally literate will be just as important as traditional literacy. Children should be taught how to navigate the internet safely, critically assess digital information, and understand the ethical implications of their online presence. Educators should introduce these concepts in an engaging way, ensuring students are well-prepared for the challenges and opportunities the digital world presents.

3. Encouraging STEM Education:

As we move further into the digital era, STEM (Science, Technology, Engineering, and Mathematics) education will become increasingly important. Schools should place a strong emphasis on these subjects, fostering curiosity and an understanding of how technology works. Encouraging students to engage in hands-on learning experiences, such as coding, robotics, and digital design, can help cultivate the next generation of innovators and problem-solvers.

4. Fostering Collaboration and Communication Skills:

While technology is essential, the ability to collaborate and communicate effectively in a digital environment is equally important. Schools should teach children how to work together using digital platforms, participate in virtual discussions, and develop strong communication skills in both online and offline settings. These abilities will be crucial in their future professional lives, where digital teamwork and remote communication will be the norm.

5. Building Adaptability and Lifelong Learning:

The future of work will require individuals to adapt to constantly changing technology. Therefore, schools should instill the values of adaptability and lifelong learning in children. By encouraging a growth mindset and a passion for learning, educators can help prepare students to continually evolve and thrive in an ever-changing digital landscape.

In conclusion, preparing children for the digital world goes beyond teaching them how to use technology. It involves fostering critical thinking, digital literacy, creativity, and collaboration to ensure they can navigate and succeed in the future digital economy. As we look ahead, education will be the key to unlocking the potential of the next generation in this exciting digital age.

References

1. Westerman, G., Bonnet, D., & McAfee, A. (2014). Leading Digital: Turning Technology into Business Transformation. Harvard Busine

2. Siebel, T. M. (2019). Digital Transformation: Survive and Thrive in an Era of Mass Extinction. RosettaBooks.

3. Rogers, D. L. (2016). The Digital Transformation Playbook: Rethink Your Business for the Digital Age. Columbia University Press.

4. Raskino, M., & Waller, G. (2016). Digital to the Core: Remastering Leadership for Your Industry. Bloomsbury Business.

5. Christensen, C. M. (1997). The Innovator's Dilemma: When New Technologies Cause Great Firms to Fail. Harvard Business Review Press.

6. Various authors. (n.d.). Digital Transformation Articles. Harvard Business Review. Retrieved from https://hbr.org

7. McKinsey & Company. (n.d.). Digital Transformation Insights. Retrieved from https://www.mckinsey.com

8. Gartner, Inc. (n.d.). Digital Maturity and Transformation Reports. Retrieved from https://

Somayeh Fakhraei

www.gartner.com

www.ingramcontent.com/pod-product-compliance
Lightning Source LLC
LaVergne TN
LVHW042350060326
832902LV00006B/518